Internet Marketing for Women

*Proven & Effective Strategies
to Grow Your Business &
Make More Money
With Social Media & Fabulous
Marketing Tools*

By
Julie Rausch

© Copyright 2017 by JRPublishingGroup - All rights reserved.

The following eBook is reproduced below with the goal of providing information that is as accurate and as reliable as possible. Regardless, purchasing this eBook can be seen as consent to the fact that both the publisher and the author of this book are in no way experts on the topics discussed within, and that any recommendations or suggestions made herein are for entertainment purposes only. Professionals should be consulted as needed before undertaking any of the action endorsed herein.

This declaration is deemed fair and valid by both the American Bar Association and the Committee of Publishers Association and is legally binding throughout the United States.

Furthermore, the transmission, duplication or reproduction of any of the following work, including precise information, will be considered an illegal act, irrespective whether it is done electronically or in print. The legality extends to creating a secondary or tertiary copy of the work or a recorded copy and is only allowed with express written consent of the Publisher. All additional rights are reserved.

The information in the following pages is broadly considered to be a truthful and accurate account of facts, and as such any inattention, use or misuse of the information in question by the reader will render any resulting actions solely under their purview. There are no scenarios in which the publisher or the original author of this work can be in any fashion deemed liable for any hardship or damages that may befall them after undertaking information described herein.

Additionally, the information found on the following pages is intended for informational purposes only and should thus be considered, universal. As befitting its nature, the information presented is without assurance regarding its continued validity or interim quality. Trademarks that mentioned are done without written consent and can in no way be considered an endorsement from the trademark holder.

CONTENTS

Introduction 1
Impact of Social Media 4
    Facebook 8
    Twitter 15
    Instagram 19
    YouTube 23
    Pinterest 26
Website Design Strategies 32
Email Marketing 44
Online Promotions 57
Conclusion 60

Go to my website Julierausch.wix.com/author to sign up for my newsletter

Introduction

Internet marketing is imperative to your business. It will help you align your business with the many ways people decide to buy things. Studies performed by companies like Gartner show there are more people who use social media and do their research on mobile apps to carry out the price and product research before making a decision. Internet marketing gives you the chance to build relationships with your existing customers and find new customers with low-cost, regular personalized communications. If you're still not convinced, here are six reasons why internet marketing is important.

Convenience – internet marketing gives you the chance to be open for business all the time without worrying about opening an actual store and paying overtime. Offering products on the internet makes it more convenient for your customers. They can browse the store online and then place an order when it is the most convenient for them.

Reach – when you market on the internet you can overcome distance barriers. You can sell your products anywhere in the country without having to open an actual store, which widens your target market. You can also build a business that can export goods without the need of numerous distributors in other countries. However, if you do choose to sell internationally, you need to use local services to know if your product will sell well with the locals and comply with city and county regulations. Localization services will let you know if you need to modify any products to show the local market and helps with translation.

Cost – internet marketing tends to cost less than marketing through physical outlets. You won't have recurring costs that come up, and you don't have to worry about any maintenance.

Personalization – you can personalize specific offers to your customers through internet marketing by keeping a profile of what they buy regularly and history. By tracking product information and web pages that prospects visit, you will be able to make targeted offers. The information you get from tracking their website visits also provides information to help with cross-selling campaigns so you can increase sales value.

Relationships – the internet gives you a great platform to build relationships with your customers and helps you keep your customer base. Once a customer has bought products from you, you can build a relationship by sending them an email that confirms the transaction. Emailing your customers with offers that are just for them helps to keep the relationship. You can also ask them to provide product reviews.

Social – internet marketing gives you the chance to be a part of the growing power of social media. Harvard Business School published an article that highlighted the link between social media and growing online revenue. According to their research, consumers responded stronger to the social network influence, which increased sales of around 5%. Take advantage of this influence by using social media as a tool to help with internet marketing.

Impact of Social Media

With social media marketing, businesses reported a 100% higher lead-to-close rate than any other market. Around 84% of all B2B marketers use social media in some way. No matter your market or product, making use of social media as a marketing tool will help you expand your brand.

At this point, not being active on social media is like having a flip phone out during a business meeting, and then complaining about the fact that your boss keeps giving somebody else all the good jobs.

Yet there are still people with flip phones, and some still buck the system and say, what is marketing through social media going to help me do? Do I have to have it? Yes. Here are some very compelling reasons why.

1. Social media helps to drive targeted traffic

Taking an amazing selfie and creating a new page on your website is pretty much the same thing. You want everybody around the world to see it, but you're not interested in begging for the attention, even worse, pay somebody for it. This is the reason why for landing pages and selfies, having social posts that are well placed makes the biggest difference. One link shared on Reddit has been able to bring more than 20,000 visitors in a single link. Websites shared to

StumbleUpon can up a page from a handful of visitors to hundreds.

2. Social media helps to boost your SEO

People who constantly use search engines know the pages that are always earning traffic and which are ignored and forgotten. A great SEO content strategy is a crucial part of getting the best spots in search engine rankings, but they will climb faster by driving traffic to your optimized pages. You can successfully drive traffic to your website or blog by utilizing social media platforms.

3. Social media can build real relationships

Part of what makes Instagram and Twitter marketing so amazing is that fact that you can so easily communicate with your customers. You can look at their updates and tweets to get information about their life. What products do they buy? What are their plans for the weekend? What posts do they like to share?

4. Users are responsive to your messages

Facebook and Twitter are viewed as social networks by most people and not tools for marketing. As a result, they won't view your posts as advertisements thus making them more open to hearing what you want to share with them. This will then turn into more web traffic when you share your link in your posts.

5. Social Media ads allow targeting and retargeting

The customizable nature of social media ads is what makes it so important. You can target certain users with Facebook ads through things like certain location, industry, purchase history, education level, and pages they've liked.

6. Problems get immediate response

If a problem with your service or product were to come up, then you will want to know about it as soon as possible. With the feedback that you will receive through social media, you will know when any issues come up.

7. Builds brand loyalty

Texas Tech University discovered that brands that had social media accounts had a larger number of loyal customers. You can easily see why: when you interact and engage with social media, they start to see you less as a corporation and more as a like-minded person or group of people.

8. The competition is social, so you should be too

91% of businesses will have more than a single social media account. This isn't a good thing to fall behind your competition on because it's going to be extremely hard to play catch up. When you're active and engaging on several networks, you will be able to gain followers and friends first, and the competition will have to play catch up.

9. Social media will get you more sales

70% of business-to-consumer marketers get their customers through Facebook, and 84% of VPs and CEOs say they use social media to make purchasing decisions.

10. It's free

You can't really argue with that logic, can you? If you control your own accounts, running social networking is about as cheap as it comes. If you hire an online PR agency or social media management, it will run you about $3000 to $7000 each month, but it will probably be an investment that you will see a return on. On a smaller scale, you can hire a virtual assistant to manage your social media. You can hire a virtual assistant on websites such as Freelancer.com or Upwork.com at fairly inexpensive rates.

Facebook

Facebook is the top social platform for businesses to use. 41% of US small businesses make use of Facebook in the marketing strategy. While it's a great marketing tool, you have to understand the best practices and strategies to see the most return.

1. Optimize your Facebook page of likes and SEO

Your page is where your marketing efforts start. Ideally, you want it to rank in Google and Facebook search so that customers can easily find you. Once they have found you, it should be appealing so people will like you.

Pick a memorable and descriptive username – Your Facebook page username is the web address for your page. As a default, you will be given a random URL made up of numbers. The username needs to convey your pages topic or your full business name accurately. You will need 25 likes to customize your vanity URL.

Descriptive keywords should be used in the About section – The About section is the main text-based real estate on a Facebook page. Make sure you use accurate, descriptive words for your products and business. Use keywords customers may use when searching for you. Adding your website URL in the description will encourage clicks to your site.

Use the appropriate category – Too often businesses choose the wrong category. This is a problem, especially if you want your page to be in the Facebook Graph Search. If you are a local business, make sure you select that as you type because this will ensure people can "check-in" at your business. If you don't have actual walk-in traffic and don't have an actual need for check-ins, picking 'Companies & Organizations' would be more appropriate.

Optimize images – Your profile and cover photos are what people see first. Your images need to be professional quality, and accurately reflect the feel and look of your brand. Optimal sizes would be 851X315 pixels for your cover photo and 160X160 pixels for your profile photo.

Make use of pinned posts – Research has found the most people will only visit your page once. They will like it, and then interact with posts that appear on their newsfeed, but will rarely visit your wall. That means your main job is to get people to click like. Facebook lets admins pin one post on their page. The topic should be unique, interesting, and contain an eye-catching image.

2. Make use of Facebook groups to engage with your market

Pages may be the primary marketing tool on Facebook; groups can be an effective add-on in many niches and industries. Groups can lead to more traffic, increased engagement, and increased authority in your niche.

When you participate in other's industry-related groups, you will be able to establish yourself as an authority in your niche. When you offer useful advice and tips, you become a valued group member. As people grow to trust you, they will want to learn more about you.

The most beneficial part of groups is to participate and create your own interest-related group. They give you the change to engage with your audience in a more personal way, and it allows you to become a part of your customer's day-to-day conversations.

3. Encourage share with Facebook Plugins and Buttons

Your Facebook page and website need to work seamlessly together. Your marketing funnel will probably work by moving Facebook traffic to your blog or website. You should also make sure that your website visitors will have a way to share and like your Facebook content.

Make sure that each piece of your content has a share and like button next to it. This can be added manually or with the use of a third party service such as WordPress or Add This plugin.

To allow your website visitors the chance interact with and like your page, install the page plugin to your site's sidebar. When you set up the plugin, it will give you options regarding how you want it to look. It's best if you choose 'Show Page Posts' so that your website visitors can preview the type of content you normally share.

4. Get your posts seen by more fans

A big complaint amongst page owners is many of their fans don't see their posts. Facebook stated that the reason for the falling reach is the result of two things: One, the sheer amount of content that is shared every day doesn't allow enough space in user's newsfeed. This makes placement a fierce competition.

The second reason is that Facebook shows the most relevant content to its users. They determine relevancy through how a person has interacted with a page, the type of post, and the page's popularity among all users. This means that the more popular your posts are, the more often they will be in your fan's feeds.

Here are some strategies to help up your chances of showing up in your fan's feeds:

- Make use of videos – research has shown that videos lead in terms of organic reach.

- Check your page insights to see the types of content that are resonating – the insights page contains a wealth of data as to what content is getting the most engagement from your audience. See the types of posts that get the most traction, as well as what your audience is passionate about.

- With promotional content, make sure to include an engaging backstory

Make sure you add plenty of engaging content to your promotional posts to make sure that it is seen.

5. How often and when to post

There are lots of business owners that get hung up on posting the perfect time, but the truth is, there isn't a one-size-fits-all approach to posting. All of the research has been done to find the optimal posting time and frequency, but this should be used as a starting point for your own research. Check your own Facebook Insights to see when your audience views posts.

Some research has found the posting on Thursdays and Friday's results in better engagement. The best posting times seem to vary, but 1 pm and 3 pm seem to be the best place to start testing.

When it comes to frequency, try to find a balance between informative and annoying. There are some businesses that do well posting five to ten times every day. For some, once a day or three times a week is appropriate. A good rule of thumb is five to ten posts a week. If you post less than two posts a week, you keep your audience engaged.

6. Paid options to increase reach and likes

While you can get a good reach through free strategies, you may want to also supplement organic strategies with paid choices.

Post boosts – when you boost a post it will increase its visibility in newsfeeds. You can choose to have the post shown to fans, fans friends, or others that you pick through targeting. This is a quick and easy way to expand the reach of your posts, but promoting your posts can be better.

Promoted posts – you can get to promoted posts through your Facebook Ads Manager. Head to the Facebook Ad Creator and click on boost your posts. This may still be called boosting; you will see more targeting and budgeting options than just clicking on a boost from your page.

7. When to promote

A hard decision you will have to make is picking the best time to promote a post. You should only promote a post that helps you to meet a specific goal, such as driving website traffic or selling something. Once you've decided to promote a post, I suggest using Jay Behr's STIR strategy. The best practice is to ask yourself a series of questions about S – shelf-life, T – timing, I – impact, R – results of a paid post.

8. Facebook Ads

Unfortunately, it's extremely easy to send out a lot of money on your ads without achieving your desired goal. Ads can be a helpful way to get conversions, traffic, and likes, but there are some practices you need to follow.

Use audience targeting – if you advertise to a general audience, you will be throwing away money. You should also test out a variety of targeting options because they tend to effective options.

Most important content first – users normally see content near the beginning of your ad. Because of this, you need to put your most important content, such as a call to action, such as "buy now", near the beginning.

Rotate ads every one to two weeks – this is especially true if you use specific targeting. You should change up your ad's copy and image every week or so. If you keep the same content, you are decreasing your chance of getting your ad noticed.

A strong call to action – always tell your users what you want them to do. While you don't have to tell them to click your ad specifically, you should tell them why they should click on it. Give them a compelling reason why they can't live without it.

Twitter

As of 2017, Twitter has an average of 330 million monthly active users. That's a lot of people that you could market to if you know how to. So what is the best way to leverage the 140-character social network to help you drive traffic to your website or business? Let's look at 14 ways to optimize your Twitter marketing.

1. Optimize your bio

You have to make sure that your company has a well-branded voice and identity. This means you need to have a bio that lets your visitors know who you are and make sure that you include a link to your landing page or website. It's important that you keep your tone consistent on everything so that people can get a sense of who you are.

2. Find the experts and influencers in your same target and engage with them on a regular basis

Make use of Twitter as a search tool to locate like-minded influencers, prospects, and customers by looking up keywords related to your niche. Follow them and interact with them daily. Create a list of the most influential people that are a part of your niche. This can include potential partners, writers, big-name bloggers, potential customers or clients, leaders, journalists, and so on. Make a private Twitter list and add them. Try to engage with them every day. Make sure you keep interactions casual and helpful. Don't sound promotional.

3. Involved colleagues

If you have more than one person in your business, then your first step is to build your brand through internal means. Make sure everybody that works with you follows you on Twitter and that they tweet, retweet, and engage with your content.

4. Tweet regularly

Regular tweets show people that you are a healthy and active profile. If you only tweet once a week or month, then people will end up forgetting about you. Daily posts and engagement are best so that you stay in your follower's mind. Make sure your content is useful and relevant.

5. Ask people for some Twitter love

Don't be afraid to ask your followers to retweet, favorite or mention your tweets, or to add your content to a fresh tweet on their page.

6. Track and respond to mentions

Keep track of your brand keywords and mentions so that you know what others are saying. Make sure that you respond politely if appropriate. Monitor their conversations and jump in at an appropriate time.

7. Retweet

Make sure that you make use of retweets. This will help to link you with leadership within your niche.

8. Favorite tweets

A lot of people don't realize that they can have favorite tweets, but it can be useful in getting someone's attention more so than a mention or a retweet.

9. Follow hashtags or trends

Take a look at what hashtags are trending and topics and figure out a way to connect them to your brand. When you can put your business within the group of trending topics, people will see your handle whenever they search for those trending hashtags. You should make sure that you use hashtags sparingly. They can easily become seen as Twitter spam when you attach them to irrelevant contents or overuse them.

10. Offer special deals or discounts to your followers

Run contests on Twitter like "The next 50 people that retweet one of my posts will get a 50 percent off coupon." You can have people post pictures of themselves using your product.

11. Use videos and images

Videos and photos can drive three to four more clicks on Twitter. Rich content has been proven to get a lot more shares and clicks than plain text tweets.

12. Use promoted tweets

Directly target your audience by using promoted tweets. If you fail to clearly state who it is you want to reach, it could end up costing you money and time. Your goal is to provide value that makes you look credible, not like you're trying to trick people into clicking your link.

13. Integrate Twitter with all your marketing efforts

Twitter is more effective when you use them along with your other marketing work. If you choose to run a contest or promotion on Twitter, let your email subscribers know about it, as they are also still an important part of your customer base. You can also periodically tweet out your mailing list link; this will allow you to tap your Twitter followers into your email list.

14. Make use of Twitter analytics

Make use of Twitter's analytics each day to help you understand what is working for your audience that you have built. When you're in the analytics dashboard, you will be able to figure out when your best days to share a tweet are, the kind of content that gets more likes, and your follower's demographics. Replicate what is working for you.

Instagram

It's definitely not a secret that a business needs to have a presence on Instagram. Instagram has more than 500 million users making is a network that provides an amazing platform for marketing to reach customers all over the world.

You will have to increase your following on a consistent and steady basis to improve your Instagram marketing. After all, the more followers that are in contact with you on Instagram, the bigger the audience you have to reach with each of your posts.

1. Make use of free Instagram tools

Instagram has implemented a business profile that resembles Facebook's business profiles, complete with a "contact" call-to-action that allows followers to text, email, or call your business.

Besides the contact button, businesses also have analytics, or Insights, that gives users a way to check their engagement and impression date. If you are interested in getting your business started with Instagram, then it is in your best interest to convert your personal account to a business account so that you can take advantage of all of their options. The better you can understand the ways that your followers interact with your content, the easier it will be to make improvements to your engagement.

2. Cross promotion

If you want to easily add followers on Instagram that are already a fan of your brand, then you should post on all of your accounts. Invite followers on Twitter or Facebook to follower you on Instagram. They already follow you, so they are interested in what your brand has to offer, so this will provide them with a different way to connect with you.

You should never assume that all of your posts reach all of the followers connected with you. A lot of people will start to move away from different platforms, and some are more active on one than they are on another. This is why you want your followers connected to as many of your social accounts as possible.

3. Don't overwhelm them

You should post often enough that you stay relevant, but not so much that you start to overwhelm your followers. This will only end up causing them to unfollow you because they feel as if you are always in their face.

There are no magic posting formulas that work for everybody. You will have to do your own tests to see how your followers respond. A good starting point is to post two posts a day and alternate the times to find out when you get the most engagement. Then you can begin to experiment with more or fewer posts each day. Make sure you pay close attention to engagement. Once you figure out your sweet spot, the testing isn't really going to stop, as the number of followers grows, you will have to make adjusts.

4. Interact with your followers

If somebody spends time leaving a comment on a post, take a couple of seconds to reply back and thank them. Just that bit of engagement can create a loyal follower, and it will also promote your brand.

Also, try incorporating things into your posts to interact with your followers. Something as simple as, "tag four friends that would love this," can expand your brand to a bigger audience, and it will provide you with new followers. Since a friend is introducing them to your profile, they are less resistance, which will result in most of the people who were tagged to follow you.

5. Make a hashtag

Coming up with an interactive hashtag is the perfect way to increase your engagement, you just need to make sure that you are correctly using those hashtags. A great way to use hashtags is to create a hashtag that customers use when they post pictures of themselves with your products.

6. Repurpose relevant content from other users

If you are finding it difficult to create enough relevant content to meet the needs of your follower's, consider repurposing the content from somebody else's Instagram. You need to make sure that you give them credit for tagging and mentioning them.

7. Use creativity to connect with your followers

When you are creative with your images, it helps you to connect with your followers. This is a more effective tactic than posting images that only look like an advertisement.

YouTube

YouTube is one of the top two search engines in the world, streaming videos to a population of people that exceed the amount of people in Indonesia, the US, and Brazil combined. With more than 100 hours of videos being added every single minute and 6 billion hours of videos being watched each month, it's definitely an amazing marketing tool that you need to take advantage of. So what is the best way to get this massive audience to get to know your business? Let's look at some tips that will help you bring in the followers.

1. Create a channel that shows what your brand is about

YouTube provides you with the chance to include your company's voice with tools that let you add logos, create a color scheme, and use custom tags. There are plenty of popular YouTube pages to view to see good examples of this; PBS is a great one to check out.

2. Make use of the right words

When somebody searches for videos, YouTube uses the keywords that you add to your video, so you want to ensure that you are as specific as possible when describing and naming your videos.

3. Add your other social profiles

You should treat your YouTube channel the same way that you treat a company website. Make sure that you include links to all of your other social media accounts.

4. Make a trailer

Come up with a two to three-minute video that helps to represent what your company is about. This gives you a chance to provide people a little glimpse into what your business is like.

5. Upload how-to videos about your service or product

People love to turn to the internet for their questions. If your service or product requires any explanation, demonstrate that through an informative video. This will also bring more traffic to your channel. If you have services and products that aren't all that complicated, you could make videos that incorporate new and fun ways to see your business. To help gain interest, an ad agency made a video that depicted a scene that people could relate to. They were able to get the attention of tens of thousands of viewers.

6. Get noticed

This is the biggest challenge for all videos. Getting the attention of billions of viewers that are searching through YouTube on any given day can be difficult. It helps to grab their attention by using an attention-grabbing image as your video's thumbnail.

7. Include testimonials

You need to establish your reputation and gain your viewers confidence by uploading testimonials you receive from customers that have used and bought your services or products. This will help potential customers to put any worries they may have to rest.

YouTube is a site that billions of people visit trying to discover new businesses like yours. Begin making use of this online resource for your business so that you can spend more time doing what you love.

Pinterest

If you believe that Twitter and Facebook are the only decent social marketing tools, then you need to think again.

Say hello to Pinterest. Pins on Pinterest are 100 times more shareable than a tweet is. On average a retweet hits only 1.4%. The half-life of a pin is 16000 times longer than a Facebook post.

Besides from its ability to feed obsessions with amazing exotic destination vacations and gorgeous foods, Pinterest's real powers are the features they provide business accounts. When you become a part of the 500,000 businesses with a Pinterest account, you will get the extra marketing features to help promote your business on a fast-growing and popular social media platform.

Creating a popular pin:

Social Media Examiner has described Pinterest as a visual search engine. Just like when you create a new article or post on Instagram, you have to make sure the content is searchable. If it can't be searched, then it won't be found or read.

The best categories – If you are educated about which categories fair well on Pinterest, then you will be able to get a better idea of what boards will work. The top ten most popular categories on Pinterest are food and drink, DIY crafts, home décor, women's fashion, other, weddings, design, hair and beauty, art, and kids. If there is no connection in your business with weddings or DIY crafts, then you shouldn't create a board for either one of the categories.

Working images – You can clearly see how visual Pinterest is. With such an emphasis on images, your images are the most important part of your pins. For a top pin, you have to have a clear, high-resolution image; these are more professional and appealing. Lighter colored images are repined 20 times more often than dark. Images that don't have faces are repinned 23% more often.

Optimal size – Every pin has to have the same width size, but their length is unlimited. The best size that you should go for is 736x1102 pixels.

Instructographics – Sometimes that unlimited length on Pinterest can come in handy. Pinterest coined the term instructographic and is pretty much the same thing as an infographic. These tend to be popular because of they are very DIY and how-to in nature, which just happens to be the second most popular category.

Getting your pins shared and seen:

Creating a fantastic pin is only part of the game. Getting your pin seen and shared is another story. Nobody will be able to locate your pin if you don't optimize if for engagement.

Posting time – Just like Facebook, Twitter, and Instagram, there are optimal times to post on Pinterest. The best time will depend on your followers, so you need to test to see what times work the best for you. For a good place to start, SocialFresh says that 8 pm and 1 am EST and 2 pm and 4 pm EST are the best posting times. HubSpot also stated that Saturday morning is THE best posting time.

Pin from your website – Place a Pin It button to the images on your website or phone app directly through Pinterest. This buttons will help to direct your website visitors to visit your Pinterest or to pin some of the content from your website to their account. If you don't use the buttons, then there isn't much chance that your site will have interaction with your Pinterest.

Connect your other accounts – It's not fun if you have to start over locating followers when you start a new social account. It's extremely easy to add your Facebook and Twitter accounts to a Pinterest account. This will help you to reach a larger amount of followers by tapping into your other social accounts that you are already established on. This helps you to share your content on several platforms, making your audience larger.

Share pins in a newsletter – Get rid of the difficulty of attracting new people to view your pins by sharing the pins with them. An email newsletter is a great way to add a couple of your most recent pins and to direct them to your account.

SEO – You have to make sure that you use SEO strategies to help your pins get discovered. Don't fret though, it won't take too much optimization for your pins. Make use of tools like Google AdWords Keyword Planner to figure out which related keywords are the most popular. Add these keywords to your pin titles and your pin descriptions. You can also add them to your pin image file name. Just like any other SEO optimization, make sure that you don't end up sounding too "keywordy." Don't over the top and add several keywords to your description and title and come off like a robot. Optimize you pin, but make sure that you still sound like a human.

Engagement to build followers and relationships:

After you can make good pins and get them seen, the next thing you need to do is to use your pins to make relationships with influencers and followers that will increase your reach. When you have more reach, you will create more success.

When you understand what other users are looking for when they follow different accounts, will ultimately help you to provide them the things they want. This will then grow your following.

In on Pinterest study, The University of Minnesota discovered that three biggest factors that Pinterest users take into consideration during their "should I follow" decision are:

- The amount of boards you have
- How many pins you have
- The number of accounts you are following and are following you

Post frequently – To grow your followers, you need to post between five to 30 new pins each day. You have to make sure that you aren't just repining things that other people have posted, but pinning unique content pins. A word of warning, don't post 30 pins within a five-minute time span. Spread out the post throughout the day. A good tip is to make a secret board. You can make all of you pins for that day and post them to the secret board, and then send them out at different times of the day.

Engage with your followers – As with Twitter, Facebook, and Instagram comment, you should engage with your followers directly by commenting back to them and answering their questions. Go the extra mile and use their names. This will bring your customer service to a new level.

Comment on other's pins – Engaging with people isn't a one-way street. You have to reach out to other follower's and their boards. Place comments on their pins so that they can feel more connected to you. It also helps that their followers will also see your brand.

Engage and follow with the most popular boards – You can learn a lot from people who have already struck gold with Pinterest. See what they pin, what boards they have, and how they engage. You want to reach their level. If you comment on their popular pins, you will be sharing your brand name with a large number of people.

Ask to join group boards. By doing this you gain their followers and grow your exposure. Most groups will be very receptive, especially if you have a lot of good content. When you go to the group board you will want to email the group's administrator whose profile will be the first circle on the top right, above the boards. Send them a friendly email asking to join their group.

Website Design Strategies

To name just a few, websites such as Wix.com, GoDaddy, and SiteBuilder.com are very user-friendly and intuitive when considering building your own website. Designing websites is not art. It does involve many different skills like art, layout, typography, and copywriting that are all stuck together to make an interface that uses features that are nice looking words but shows functionality and ease of access to the content it features.

To be able to combine all of these elements together and get results you need a clear direction. These directions should guide all aspects of the design to one common goal. You need to think strategically.

You are probably wondering what strategic design is. Strategic design happens when you fuse your goals with all aspects of the design process. You are not just designing an interface that is accessible, usable and looks good. You are designing one that will allow you to accomplish your objectives.

Many websites look great and incorporate all the latest gadgets into their design by fail horrible with their function. Don't get me wrong; design trends are important since they give us new techniques and inspiration. Implementing these styles and techniques must be focused and intelligent. Don't try to market on your blog. You need to focus on readability and usability instead of style. Websites that promote games need to feature graphics and things that give off a certain style and feel. Aesthetics are very important.

If a designer only uses a feel and look that works for one certain moment in time without giving any thought to how well it will function, the results will not be very effective.

Designing a website is about making an interface that is accessible, usable, and functions properly. It will also give off the correct feelings and emotions. All these elements are needed to get in touch with your businesses goals and stay in sync with your objectives. You need to identify these goals and use them to help with your design.

Here are some ways to help you think strategically about your website design:

Figure Out Your Goals

The first thing you should do before you start working on the design of your website is to know what your goals are. What do you want to achieve with this design? What is the purpose of the website? Ask yourself, a manager, or a client what these are. If you or they can't answer this question, you need to talk to someone until everything is agreed upon. Having clear directions is necessary if your design is to have a purpose.

Websites are works of art. It is an interface that is supposed to serve a certain function. This function might be selling products, delivering information, entertaining, informing or providing a service. Whatever the function is, the design needs to fulfill it. Goals are crucial if you start to work on a redesign. Why do you need a redesign? Are you looking to grow your sign-ups, increase participation, or decrease bounce rates?

Know Your Audience

The audience plays a huge role in how your site needs to function and look. A lot of different demographics will influence your design like technical competency, profession, gender, and age. A website for a serious business journal needs a style that is different than a computer game website. Usability plays a huge role for audiences that are less tech-savvy or older.

Your audience will influence the aesthetics of the site and will determine many of the little details such font size. You need to be clear about who could end up viewing your website.

Think About Brand Image

Many designers become overly inspired by the newest trends and start using them without thinking about what their image is and if it works for their brand. Reflective floors, gradients, and glossy buttons might work on some sites, but it may not for yours.

Think color. What feelings and emotions do you want to send to others? Your design needs to show the character and personality of your business. Everybody has their own brand. It doesn't matter if you sell a service or product, the website will have a certain feel that will make a good impression on visitors to your site. Figure out what that impression needs to be.

Goal-Driven Design

You have figured out the reasons behind your website, set your goals, figured out your audience and you know your image. Now you need to use it. How will you make sure your decisions work with your strategy? Look at it this way:

If the main objective is increasing how many subscribers your website gets. How could your design help you with this? There are three things that can help:

- Make your about section as concise and clear as you can. Don't confuse visitors about functions on your website.

- Use contrast and color to make a link that stands out. If they aren't able to find your registration link, you won't be able to get anyone to sign up.

- Make the process of registration easy by getting rid of optional and unnecessary elements. They can get to those later. If the form is too long, it will turn people away.

These are just some ways you can get your design to help you accomplish your goals by increasing how many people sign up for your services. Goals might change, but strategy stays the same. Focus and shape the design elements to meet these goals.

This strategy applies to your audience and brand. Design it to suit you. If your business is entertainment, then give your audience an "experience." You can use as much or as little imagery and color as you would like. If you are creating a website focused on information, your focus should be on readability and usability. The interface should fade away so that the user doesn't get distracted by the content.

New visitors might stay on the site for just a few seconds; you need to be concise, so you don't lose them. You can accomplish this by:

- Making use of large diagrams and imagery to how your service or product works.

- Show screenshots of the application process. People prefer to know what they are getting into before that choose to sign up.

- Give a tour. Show them the different way that your service can solve their problems.

Post a video. The less effort it takes for people to understand and use your app the better.

- They need to be able to use the sign-up link on every page.

For your website to succeed it need to grab the attention of your visitors by educating and informing them quickly about your product and selling them on the benefits it gives.

Measure Your Results

After you have designed and posted your website, now you need to measure the success. This is important since you won't know how effective the design is until you test it out.

If you wanted to increase how many sign ups you get, measure to see if the changes made a positive impact. If your goal was to increase subscribers to your blog, you could check this by looking at RSS stats. If your goal was to increase involvement, check your comments to see if they have increased.

You could ask for feedback. This is the perfect way for you to see if you are going the right way. Just don't try to implement all the suggestions that people give you. Everybody has different tastes so everybody will also have different opinions about how the website should look. After you have collected feedback, check for patterns and see if you have any common issues that keep popping. Make these changes first.

Measuring website metrics is a complete science all by itself. It really doesn't matter how in-depth the analytics are right now, the main thing is you have some way to measure your objectives. Use the information to make sure your design is moving you in the right direction.

Kaizen

The Japanese philosophy of Kaizen puts the focus on small steps to continuously improve. When working on your website, think about Kaizen since what you just posted won't be your final version. You don't even need a final version.

You can constantly make improvements, and the way that a website works allows you to implement these at whatever time you need to. Since a website is not like a magazine that once it goes to print, you can't change anything or fix problems. With a website, it stays on your computer. If you screw something up, you can change it. You can also introduce improvements gradually and update your website to make it more efficient.

Using the measurement results, you will be able to see where the problem areas are. Your visitors might not be able to find the RSS link. You have a high bounce rate. You most important webpage isn't getting the right amount of traffic. It doesn't matter what the problem is, you can always fix it and improve on it.

Responsive Design

You need to make sure that your design can adjust from one device to another. This looks like a good approach, but it doesn't take into account images and text. What looks good on a desktop computer might be disastrous on mobile devices. Take your time and create a layout that works will every device. Remember to redesign images for small screens. A banner that has text might look great on a normal computer, but it might not be readable on a cell phone. You also don't want to use exactly the same images for a computer as a mobile device. The image will be scaled, but it will be larger than needed. It will increase how much bandwidth is used and how long it takes to load.

Software Prototyping

Using a graphics program like Adobe Edge Reflow to experiment with designs will help a great deal. When you have created a design that you love, you can copy the code to use with your actual layout.

A Team

You must have people that work well together. It is a good idea to have several team members if you have a lot of coding and design going on. A company I work with often has about 18 members so they can take on numerous projects at any time. This makes sure that all projects can be handled in a timely manner.

Versatility

Your team needs to be able to handle every aspect of graphic design and coding. They need to be easily accessible whether they work in an office or at home. This keeps you from being blindsided by someone that wants a certain type of job, and you don't have anyone who can do it. You will either have to run around to find support or turn the job down.

Customization

Utilizing templates might be tempting. These create a "look" that might appeal to you, especially if you deal with many corporate clients. By creating a look that is unique will make the client feel important since it helps with their branding.

Be Aware of the Marketplace

If you design for iOS, you won't have to build as many versions as you would for Android. This will simplify the process and lower cost.

Find Inspiration

You don't have to design in a vacuum. This actually makes designing harder. Look at websites that bring you inspiration. Study them and see what stands out to you. You can use these to build one of your own. You can also look for things that inspire you offline like in books and magazines. Find layout ideas that spark your creativity. When you are creating designs, be sure you do many different mockups for a client to look at. By doing this, you will have others they can choose from if they find one they don't like.

Take a Step Back

A good strategy is to step away from the screen. Most of the time, designers are working too close to their screen. Aside from the posture problems, this wreaks havoc with designs. Stepping away from the screen just for a few minutes or just moving your chair away from the desk will allow you to see the screen with different eyes. At times, elements that don't seem to go well together will look fine if you look at them from a distance. It is also a good idea to just walk away for a bit. When you come back to it, you will be able to look at it with a fresh perspective.

Start Your Design at a New Place

Most designers will start at the top of the page and work their way down. A different approach is to just experiment with blocks of design, text, and color. This makes the header just one of many components.

Test and Validate

Test your code, validate your code, and test the layout for the different devices and browsers that you have made the design for. For mobile devices, you need to turn the device sideways to see what happens to the layout.

To Sum It All Up

Everything on the web evolves. Remember that what works for this layout might not work for the next. Some design aspects won't change much and using them gives you a great foundation to start with.

The most important aspect of design work is to use common sense. You are designing something for someone who has a certain vision. It needs to fulfill that purpose. It is easy to get off track of your goals and to create something gorgeous, but it won't work within your context. It's also easy to fall into the latest trend trap, and only using things because they are pretty. These might not actually fit with what your project is about.

Try not to fall into the traps and think through each decision. Why is this button placed here? What were the tabs for? Why are the icons there? If you can train your brain to work this way, the process becomes more focused. Keep in mind the organization or product you represent. Think about the brand or audience. What works in the context? What do they expect? How can design fulfill the vision of the website? Don't just make a pretty website, create that works for your customers.

Email Marketing

There are over 205 billion emails that are sent every day. This number is thought to increase to 246 billion by the year 2019. The strategies for email marketing has changed. The strategies that worked five years ago don't work now. It is still a great component of any marketing strategy. The best online marketers are still using email marketing as their go to. Why? It brings results and delivers the best return on investment.

You read that right. Email marketing does better than search engine optimization, pay per click, and content marketing all put together. Having a great email marketing strategy is the most important part of any marketing strategy. Email is the cheapest way to promote products, reach your goals, and talk to customers. For each dollar you spend on email marketing, you will get a return of $48. Pretty good, right? Here are five ways to use email marketing to get amazing results.

Personalize Messages

Personalized email marketing doesn't mean you send email to each subscriber. Personalization is using the customer's information to send messages personally. A great example of a company that personalizes email is Amazon. Every email from Amazon is personalized. It doesn't begin with Dear Customer. It starts with "Dear Sue." They don't randomly generate suggestions. They use your buying history to show you similar products.

With Amazon, email marketing isn't another marketing channel. It is the key to a great customer experience. Amazon's CEO is a genius when it comes to email marketing. He understands how valuable emails are and will read through any customer's complaints. This is why 35 percent of sales come from customer recommendations.

Amazon isn't the only company that gets these results by using personalization. Experian did a study and found that personalized emails gave them transaction rates that were six times higher.

Let's talk numbers anyone can understand. Most email marketing will generate about 11 cents for each email. If you send out 100,000 emails, you could see around $11,000 in sales. If you were to personalize the emails, you could get six times more back in returns. Now that's a great revenue opportunity.

Around 70 percent of businesses don't use personalized emails. If you personalize your emails, you could easily stand up against your competition and win. The easiest way to personalize your emails is addressing your recipient by name. Many email service providers offer this function. This alone will increase your company's performance. An email subject line with the recipient's name will increase rates by 16 percent.

If you consider that 47 percent of most emails are opened because what's in the subject line, this is a great way to get more eyes to your emails.

Here are other tips that you can use along with the customer's name to help you with personalization:

- Get the correct information, to begin with: Personalization begins before you ever hit the send button. It begins when a person fills out your sign up form. If you don't get their info like location, company, and name, you will be extremely limited when you try to personalize your communication attempts. Just ask for what you need instead of what you want. This is just one way that general data protection regulation will impact marketing.

- Use an email that they can reply to: If you use a donotreply@blah.com, it takes away any personalization from your messages. If you want your recipients to respond and be engaged, use a real reply address to improve your credibility to show that you are personable.

- Use your authentic email signature: This goes with using a real reply to email. You must use real contact information inside your email and give them the best way they can contact you. Give your recipients an opportunity to get in touch with you or connect with you online. It is a wonderful way to build relationships and get personal with them.

Segment Subscribers

Email marketers say that segmentation is next on the list of initiatives. When you segment your database, email campaigns will be targeted toward your audience.

Look at this example:

You want to host an event to network with small businesses that are located within a 20 miles radius around you. How do you get them to come to your event? Segmentation.

The easiest way to get the owners to come to your event is to create a segment of people that call themselves small business owners that live within your radius and send them an email invite. Segmentation is simple and is done with customer relationship management software.

Think about sending emails to your whole database. You probably have subscribers all over the country possibly continent. How would you like to get an invitation to an event that is being held in another country? You probably wouldn't. Neither will they. Before you begin segmenting your database, let's see just how valuable it really is.

One study showed that all email marketing key performance indicators performed better when segmenting an email list. When you segment your lists, you will get more customers, better transactions, leads, revenue, and open rates. You may be asking if this really works? The answer is simply, yes.

If you send out two different email campaigns, both with the same subject line and content. The first was sent to a non-segmented list and the second was sent to a segmented list by interest. The non-segmented emails showed a 42 percent open rate and a 4.5 percent click-through rate. The segmented emails showed a 94 percent open rate and 38 percent click-through rate. That's pretty impressive. Is this why marketers segment their emails? No. Nine out of ten marketers don't segment their emails.

Here are some ways to get started with segmentation:

- Industry: Do you have products and services that other consumers and businesses could use? Knowing your subscriber's industry is the best way to segment your emails. If your business sells parts for cars, you would see a higher rate if you send emails to places that sell products for cars as compared to businesses that cell phones.

- Company size: Segmenting emails by annual revenue or company size is a wonderful way to increase rates. A business that only has five employees isn't going to want to go to a big industry conference, but a business who employs 750 people would be more likely to go to it.
- Sales cycle: Early buyers are not going to be ready for aggressive sales pitches or one on one demos, but they would appreciate receiving industry research on paper. On the other hand, buyers that are ready will respond to free trial offers or product webinars.

Send Emails that are Mobile Friendly

There is about 54 percent of the mobile users in the world who will open their email on their mobile devices. This is a fairly large number. What is the first thing you do in the morning? You reach for your phone and check it for email, messages, and missed calls.

About 62 percent of all mobile users do this. If you send an email to someone who opens it on their mobile devices, but the email hasn't been optimized for mobile devices, what are they going to do?

The first thing they will likely do is to unsubscribe and delete it. Why are half of all emails, not mobile friendly? When emails that are optimized for mobile devices generate much more revenue. The average revenue generated by mobile email is 40 cents per email. This is about four times greater than what desktop emails bring in.

Almost 55 percent of all smartphone users have purchased their mobile devices after receiving an email. About 36 percent of all business to business companies have optimized their emails to be viewed on mobile devices. They saw an improvement in the email performance.

How can you optimize your emails for mobile users?

- Implement responsive email design: Creating a RED design means the user's email is optimized no matter what device they are using. Most email service providers offer a solution in their email functions.

- Keep the pre-header and subject line short: Subject lines are critical. Keep it short, so the recipient knows what the email is about. The pre-header text shouldn't be wasted by saying "To view this email...." Try to summarize or use a call to action like giving them a coupon for free shipping.

- The Call to Action needs to be Obvious and Big: Mobile devices are all different sizes. If a text link works on a device with large screens, you could be alienating readers who have small devices or large hands. If you CTA is very small, make it bold, big, and easy to click.

Buttons, Design, and Test Copy

You need to test your email templates, landing page, and home pages. Testing gives you data to make decisions that improve your marketing performance. Email marketing isn't any different. You have tested subject lines, who hasn't.

If you send out different variations of the subject line to different subscribers, you can calculate the amount of revenue you can expect to receive. A sample revealed that the weakest line would generate about $400,000. The best line was thought to being $2,500,000. That is huge.

You can test other things by email marketing:

- From address: What appears in the form field has a great impact on if the reader will open the email or not. The sender name is the reason why the email gets opened. Test the *from address* by sending it from your CEO, company plus person, or just a person.

- HTML vs. Plain Text: Like many marketers, you send out plain texts of your emails. Have you ever thought of testing them as plain text only? When you add personalization, these emails look like they were written just for the recipient.

- Short vs. Long Emails: You have the option of sending out emails that are short or long. Long emails will include more detailed copies where short emails will send the recipient straight to a landing page. This way you can see which one works best.

Automate Emails When Possible

Trigger emails are sent out automatically based on the user's behavior. The most common are welcome, transactional, and thank you emails. Think about emails you get when you order something like order confirmation and receipts sent to your email. Trigger emails perform better than normal emails.

One study showed:

- Trigger emails open rates average about 49 percent. This is 95 percent higher than normal email.
- Trigger emails click-through rate is doubled when compared to normal email.
- Sites that convert about 40 percent of their traffic use trigger email.

Trigger-based email campaigns will generate four times more revenue and 18 times more profits. It does sound too good to be true. It has been tested, and it works.

About 25 percent of today's marketers use triggered emails and make up about 2.6 percent of the overall email volume. They are responsible for 20 percent of your revenue. Trigger emails work well since they hit an email marketing sweet spot.

Think about this:

You see an ad on social media and go to their website, you add an item to the cart but decide to leave before finishing the purchase. This happens a lot, every day. You check your email an hour later and have an email that shows the product you were thinking about buying along with a coupon for a ten percent discount plus free shipping. You are enticed to complete the purchase. This is the power of trigger emails.

Setting up triggered emails isn't that complex or expensive. You could start by using autoresponders with your customer service software.

Here are examples of trigger emails you can use:

- Activation: A user creates an account but doesn't come back to your site within a week. You can create an activation campaign that will send automated emails with their information along with steps on how to get started. You can even include a video to demonstrate for added support. Invite them to a meeting and walk them through any problems they may be having. Answer their questions in a timely manner.

- Win-back: A customer is getting near the end of their subscription. They haven't used the product for the past three months, and you need to get them back and keep them for one more year. Make a win-back email that will send automated emails to every customer that is coming to the end of their contract. Give them a list of new products and features along with a short plan of expected releases within the next few months.

- Surprise: Loyal customers are the key to success. You should reward your loyal customers by offering free products or services. Send them a surprise email that offers them a coupon for free doughnuts, cupcakes, gift cards, or even a free year to your software. It is a cost for the company, but the rewards will be big.

Email marketing will deliver results. Email marketing has evolved over the years. It isn't just as simple as sending the exact same email to everyone. You need to update your marketing strategy. You need to send targeted messages. Personalized messages that can be opened on any device.

Test new elements. Trends quickly change and what worked last month may not work today.

When you have figured out what works, find a way to automate with triggered emails.

When you can make these new changes, your customers will become more responsive. Your performance will improve, and you will see your business grow.

The Best Time to Send Emails

There are numerous emails sent out during business hours, the ones that have the best open rates are not sent between 9 am and 5 pm. The best email strategy is to send emails at night. These emails should be sent between 8 pm and midnight. This block outperforms all times for open rates, click-throughs, and sales. This window is not used as much, and this helps the late night emails outperform.

The time for optimal mailing will depend on the consumer's behavior, inbox crowding, and when other marketers send out their emails.

Deployment times and inbox crowding of marketers go hand in hand. If your email gets sent out at times when there aren't many others sent, it will have a better chance of being seen.

Optimal emailing to customers is totally up to you. Do a lot of testing and figure out how your customers tick and when they open their email.

Email is Used More than Twitter and Facebook

Social media might be nipping on email's heels, but the inbox still holds its own to social influence. SocialTwist did a study over an 18-month time frame. They monitored 119 campaigns from leading companies and brands. Their results showed an advantage to the ability of email to get new customers as compared to Twitter and Facebook.

Out of the 300,000 people that became customers, 50.8 percent was gotten through email. Twitter reached 26.8 percent, and Facebook gained 22 percent.

Email rules by double. Mailchimp, Aweber, and Constant Contact are a few email marketing service providers with intuitive platforms.

Email on the Weekend

Sending emails on Saturday and Sunday outperform any weekday emails. The amount of email that is sent over the weekend is low just like the late evening email. These can help your messages stand out even more. The rates for sales, open, and click through aren't substantial, but in marketing, every bit counts.

Online Promotions

To be able to increase your business's growth, you must increase people's awareness and get them engaged online. Using promotions like sweepstakes, giveaways, and contest are the best tools you could use to build excitement about your business. It can also help you build better relationships with existing and potential customers in miraculous ways.

Here are some tips to make sure your next promotion is a rousing success:

- Make Participations Very Easy: If you can make it extremely easy for people to get involved with your promotions, and the prizes are exceptional, they will get involved quicker. To get the best participation, get rid of all the barriers you can. Making them jump through hoops like making them create an account or the entry form is numerous pages long will decrease the chances of them entering. Remember the old adage, keep it simple. Creating a promotion that is complex might seem like fun for you, but for customers, the easier the process, the more people you will attract.
- Share Photos: By placing photos in your promotion is a great way to get your audience engaged. Consumers enjoy

looking at photos when spending time with friends whether it is in person or on social media. Potential clients will engage faster with businesses if they place photos on their site. People love to look at photos. They also love to show off their skills. Increase their engagement by letting them share a photo as a way to enter your contest.

- Promotions Need to be Mobile-Friendly: Around 66 percent of promotions are viewed on mobile devices. Since most people use their mobile devices and smartphones for everything, you need to think about how your promotion will look on all mobile devices. You can't just shrink it to fit; you must adapt it to work on all mobile devices. Some platforms can detect what browser is being used and will optimize your promotion for each device.

- Use Word-of-Mouth to Fuel Your Promotion: For each person that entered a competition, there were 3.6 more people who entered due to social sharing. Ask your staff and clients to share the promotion on the social media they use. Contests on Twitter asks users to retweet the contest as a way to enter, and this shares the contest with other Twitter users. Offer your staff click-to-tweets to get awareness out there quickly and easily. If you are promoting on Facebook, do the same thing with a share button. Just remember to add a disclosure if your employees share.

- Supercharge the Promotion by Using Paid Media: You must invest in your promotion to succeed. Use the leverage of Facebook's promoted posts, sponsored stories, and ads. This is an affordable and great way to reach farther than just the people who are already following you. Paid StumbleUpon ads, LinkedIn ads, and promoted tweets will increase participation. Paid media can increase participation by about 55 percent and lowers the cost per entry by about 42 percent.

Using social media to bring awareness to your promotion are key for any marketer. Get the most out of them by making sure they are mobile, promoted, shareable, engaging, and simple. Remember to optimize your reach by increasing your chances of people talking about it. Most important, make sure you are worthy of being talked about.

Conclusion

Thank you for reading through to the end of *Internet Marketing for Women*. Let's hope it was informative and able to provide you with all of the tools you need to achieve your goals.

The next step is to start using these proven strategies to help build your business. Internet marketing is the perfect way to build your business, so it shouldn't be something that you skimp on. Every bit of marketing helps, so try out these strategies to see what works best for you.

Finally, if you found this book useful in any way, a review on Amazon is always appreciated!

Please click below to receive tips, resources, and **FREEBIES!**

Sign up on my website below.

Contact Information:

Email: julie@jrpublishinggroup.com

Website: www.julierausch.wix.com/author

www.ingramcontent.com/pod-product-compliance
Lightning Source LLC
Chambersburg PA
CBHW031546210526
45464CB00003B/1168